LIFE SCE
VERS

LAURIE WILKINSON
The Psychy Poet

This edition published in Great Britain in 2016 by

MyVoice Publishing
Ubud, Bali

ISBN 978-1-909359-54-3

'Laurie takes poetry to places other poets don't go and can't reach.'

Acknowledgements

As this is now my fourth book in a relatively short time, I will avoid too much repetition of thanks to people such as my family and friends that I regularly thank face to face anyway.

I do though humbly recognise support, compliments and encouragement, that is so important, from various people in locations near and far! Thus I briefly mention Suanne P in South Africa, Gina at Leaf Hall Seaside, & Louise C R amongst others for their feedback and advice. Of course most acknowledged folks in my previous books continue to be around for me.

I will also mention some groups, a couple again, including Anderida Writers , 42nd Highland Regiment (1815) Napoleonic re enactment group, The Best of Eastbourne networking organisation, & Polegate Business Club who have supported, promoted me and bought my books, as have my many friends again at my French Mobile Home site.

A special thanks this time to My Voice Publishing who have helped me all round to produce this and my other books, whilst enduring the fact that my technology skills are easily surpassed by the evident success of my poetry writing and book sales.

As ever my final recognition of gratitude is to people taking the time to read this book, and with an even bigger thanks to the kind folks who have bought my previous books, and will buy this one too, which ensures my donation to the excellent charity Help for Heroes from all sales again.

Introduction

This is my fourth book in two and a half years, and as I wrote in the Introductions of the previous two books I was stunned by the continued publications and their subsequent success. With this fourth book I am almost lost for words. Almost but not quite, but especially surprised as this latest book is considerably larger too!

The extra twenty five poems perhaps reflects my continued prolific writing that totals some 230 + poems written in under three years. I am very happy that they keep coming and still follow my four sections of romance, humour, reflection and tragedy, which positive feedback confirms popularity with readers.

Possibly a clue to my rolling production line is a service I offer to people to write a personalised poem for them. This is a specific verse for their family, event or business.

During the year since October 2015 I have continued to be busy in other ways, writing a monthly column with poems for two online newspapers, The Sussex Newspaper and Bonjour France which is for English speakers in France. I had a regular "The Psychy Poet Presents" slot on local radio and am hopeful of an even wider audience opportunity on radio again soon! I also make many and varied appearances reading my poetry, and the local library group have bought my three previous books.

All this is compounded by my fourth poem consecutively to be in a National final and published in The Forward Poetry book out this coming November, after a third poem was published by them in May 2016. All an excellent recognition of what I'm trying to portray to a larger readership and also to promote Help for Heroes charity.

To conclude I will say that my style has not changed, and people have kindly fed back with "improving and practised" comments on my work which is very satisfying. Please enjoy this, my fourth book and "The Journey Continues!"....

Laurie Wilkinson Bsc (hons) RMN

CONTENTS

ROMANCE

HUMOUR

REFLECTION

TRAGEDY

Laurie Wilkinson

Life Scenes

Life's scenes are acted out
Right before my eyes,
So I can't help but notice
The careless and the wise.

Thus I will have my feelings
About all that I have seen,
And I will put them into words
So others know what I mean.

For poets have passionate thoughts
Put into burning words and verse,
As I observe the world's scenes
That are better or much worse.

--ooOoo--

Laurie Wilkinson

ROMANCE

Jigsaw

Dreamy figures of great delight
All come dancing into view,
I have a panorama of beauty
But know what I must do.

For you have made intrusions
Seismic like upon my soul,
As we determine to be together
Making our separate pieces whole,
Like some closely fitting jigsaw
That a glorious picture makes,
For it had become quite desperate
To complete for both our sakes.

I can still see your posture
With majestic desire for me,
That I had to return with vigour
How it was designed to be.
Now disappearing from all else
Except the views fixed in our sight,
We released basic desires
With erupting volcano might.

So now our jigsaw was complete
And you in your ecstasy cried,
Whilst we had flown together
Returning to land satisfied.

--ooOoo--

Laurie Wilkinson

Desired Effect

In your dreams and imagination
You can conjure perfect sight.
So fashioned just for you,
It's sure to fit you right
Up your street and in your door,
As if by magic it arrived,
Delivered just for you
To ensure your wish survived.

Fantasies and pictured visions
You would like to have with you,
Can be brought to walk along
Just as if they were all true.
For the powers of want and need
May fan desires into flame,
So wish for your sensations
Without a hint of shame.

Thus have no fear of calling
Unseen icons to your mind,
Perhaps of people not yet met
Who would be nice to find.
For inside our rampant brain
Our ideas can ebb and flow,
Allowing all perceptions in
To where you want to go.

-ooOoo--

Kiss

A quiet, simmering, burning fuse
Maybe oh so easy to miss,
As with a soft awakening
To someone you'd love to kiss.
So the signs of any recognition
Or consent given from your muse,
Are sought for their confirmation
You are the one they choose.

Thus with heartbeats all a flutter
You slowly pucker up to brush,
That alluring sirens ready mouth
As you prepare to make them blush,
With that soft sweet sensation
Now blowing bubbles on your lips.
So you lean closer in together
Lest this precious moment slips.

Eyes tight shut to keep out the world
From your very own embrace,
Your bodies pulse fast and close
So you are now lost in space.
With bright stars and planets forming
Brilliant lights across the sky,
To transform your understanding
That you've just learnt to fly.

--ooOoo--

Laurie Wilkinson

Rain Dance

I saw you on the dance floor
And it seemed like it was raining.
We all felt we were getting wet
But no one was complaining,
As you went through your moves
Of your sublime sensual dance.
For everyone gaped spellbound
In their own erotic trance.

For me though it was eerie
As I had seen you in my dreams.
Knowing you would come sometime,
Least that's the way it seems.
For I felt that you were here now
For only me, and me alone,
And now I had to find resolve
To reap what I had sown.

Because I believed you heard
When I was calling out for you,
Although I didn't know your name
I knew my dream would come true.
So I stepped boldly forward
And scooped you in my arms,
Relieved to find you dry
As I was dazzled by your charms.

Thus now we are a pair
Though we often become as one,
Brought into a stark reality
In our world of constant sun.
But It's a wonder how I knew you
From my dreams fleeting glance,
Showing only rain soaked movements
That made me take my chance.

--ooOoo--

Close

Close is an intimate nearness
Of two bodies tight together.
And when that's me with you
I don't think that I could ever
Consider the heartache and pain
Of ever being torn apart,
From all your warm soft contours
Or the kindness of your heart.

So allow me to snuggle up
And encompass us both and hold
You in my passionate embrace
That all inhibitions will unfold.
Leading to those sensations
From pulsing of passions flame,
Sparked off by our desires
We must release without shame.

With our lips exploring secrets
And wonders that they find,
Amongst the sensual closeness
Of the intense lovers grind.
Following all those emotions
That a close bonding feeds,
Until volcanic movements cease
With the conclusion of our needs.

For now we have uncovered
The secrets of close touch,
So will practice continually
For we can never have too much.

--ooOoo--

Laurie Wilkinson

Lisa

Now Lisa is one of the singers
In our entertainment team.
A lovely lass from Ireland
And in many a man's dream,
With her big warming smile
And a twinkle in her eye,
That always makes you cheerful
If you see her walking by.

She also does a lot of dancing
As the team put on a show.
With synchronised dance movements
That they really have to know,
As part of a very busy day
Including looking after kids.
Which is quite often a big task
Involving many escaping bids!

But I like to hear Lisa singing
And sometimes favourite songs of mine,
So if I hear one of my special ones
I am glued to every line,
That she sings out with great gusto
As she puts every bit of her in,
For Lisa believes that not to
Is a kind of cheating sin.

But mostly I value Lisa's friendship
And with my poetry she's a fan,
So when complimenting me on this
I know I'm a lucky man.

--ooOoo--

Cut Loose

It may take time before you feel
The endings of your strife
And trembling release of pent up needs,
Freeing frustrations from your life.

So gasping from all the excitement
Brand new excursions can bring,
You will lay down breathless
Whilst heartbeat joys still sing,
Of skin touches, that made you gasp
And brought sleeping nerves alive.
Ensuring that your desired vibes
Would all very soon arrive.

But why were you so lost in sleep
That you took so long to wake?
Perhaps you were just not aware
Of sacrifices you must make.
For nothing comes from nothing
Unless you determine now to try,
To let all those trapped emotions go
Released with ecstatic sigh.

So relax and welcome sensations
Exploding in body and mind,
That maybe never reached the heights
Of these vibrant present kind,
That overcame the long journey
To climb to the very top.
And knowing that if you allow,
They may never, ever stop!

--ooOoo--

Laurie Wilkinson

Return Flight

There are some loves that will not die
Although they shouldn't really last,
But linger on still flickering
From times left in the past.

Illicit times or stolen moments
Perhaps your first real kiss,
But every now and then in life
Those memories will be missed.
For as every dog will have its day
We must all find time to fly,
Then reach out to touch the stars
At least once before we die.

With skipping heart and infants smile
And stomach churning fit to burst,
You soar and glide effortlessly
Around sensations not rehearsed.

Though every flight will end sometime
Bringing its cargo back to land,
And so you must return to life
Maybe your soul won't understand.
For we can never eternally visit
Ecstatic playing fields of gods
And even if we feel we do
It's only when the devil nods!

Thus glowing embers of loves fires
May burn against the rule,
And play on heartstrings silent now
But better than never played at all.

--ooOoo--

M N C

I was invited to Mumpreneurs Networking club
The last meeting of the departing Janine,
Who had managed the group, but is now off
For a life in Spain with a sunnier scene.
She was inundated with flowers and gifts
And a nice speech from new manager Kerry,
Who despite a sadness and nearly tears
Did her best to keep the gathering merry.

I personally was a bit taken back there
By a vibrant group of determined souls.
Who whilst very friendly and glamorous too
Were all determinedly keen on their goals,
To establish themselves in their own fields
And a varying entrepreneurial slant,
Though laughing and enjoying themselves
I could see there was no word like can't!

Thus I have willingly agreed to join up
With this bubbly, enthusiastic throng,
Who are committed to help everyone out
And push any faltering member along.

I have a feeling this will all be fun
Though where it leads me I'm not so sure,
But I have seen with this lovely lot already
That I will want to come back for more.

--ooOoo--

Laurie Wilkinson

Buried Treasure?

Are there unknown longings in you dreams
For precious moments that were missed?
With unfulfilled exploits that passed by
When your lips weren't even kissed.

Bubbling passions, fires of need
Will disturb everyone some time,
They may overshadow or negate
When your love was so sublime,
And took you dancing to the stars
Amongst the planets and the moon.
But like a rainbow in the dusk
It passed by much too soon.

So back to earth and the wee small hours
And haunting regrets come out to play,
Teasing your conscience and resolve
However hard you pray.

Deepest feelings, buried low
Will always start to rise,
Tantalising all your claims
That you won the greatest prize.

So sleep, coax or conjure
All you want, for your hearts desires.
For if you can't do this at night
They will drown in daytime mires!

--ooOoo--

Laurie Wilkinson

Lost for Words

Lizoo runs the bar at my place
A very nice and lovely French miss,
She always gives me a big welcome
With a warm smile and a kiss.

We often have a laugh with mime
But the truth makes my fists clench,
For she speaks no English at all
And I speak very little French!

There are things we try to share
With so much we would like to say,
About how life is going for us
And all the happenings of the day.

Different languages are a frustration
When they won't allow you to converse,
So you are reduced to hand gestures
Which sometimes can be worse.
But Lizoo and I have laughed too
When with more actions than spiel,
And had panic stricken realisation
We might be on security camera reel.

But good friends will always connect
With hugs, kisses or loving caress,
When we meet and have a cuddle
And these actions do us bless.

--ooOoo--

Laurie Wilkinson

Sleep Perchance?

We all love and need our sleep
Perchance to dream as the bard said,
So just relax and prepare to rest
When you put yourself to bed.

For sleep they say, is a great healer
And recharges both body and mind,
To feel refreshed in a healthy way
Maybe to solve problems too, I find.
For we're also advised in life
To "sleep on" a decision I hear,
But whether this is true or not
In the morning things seem clear.

Thus allow yourself to drift away
And to slip into a world of dreams,
Maybe to caress those hidden thoughts
So all will not be as it seems.
Then allow the visions of your deep
To take you soaring to the moon,
In a fluttering of warm sensations
You awaken from much too soon.

So just relax and prepare to escape
When laying down to sleep,
For if you can lose yourself in peace
Great councils you will keep.

--ooOoo--

Cut and Run

Just run away with me then
Drop it all and off we go,
Just look at now and move forward
To feelings and places we don't know.

Come and leave it all behind
They are only possessions anyway.
For we can't take them with us
And when we die those things all stay,
Alongside all that grief and woe
That we never did sign up for.
So that makes it so much easier
To just leave and shut the door.

Let us disappear hand in hand
Before we hear what people say,
For they won't ever understand us
Like Romeo and Juliet's of our day,
And unlike them we've seen life
So know how hard it can be.
Whilst they were besotted innocents
We are older, and must be free.

Oh I can hear the gossips scream
That we are selfish and just not fair,
But that is mostly a jealous cry
As to leave they wouldn't dare.

Then off we go my lovely siren
Away to see what will befall,
For we don't want a little sometimes
We want it now and must have it all.

And so now the deed is complete
There can be no going back.
We have eased our bodies together
Thus no sensations did we lack,
As our precious time we served
Doing all for the others sake.
But we know sadly it will be gone
When from our dream we will awake!

Laurie Wilkinson

Alluring Lynsey

Lovely Lynsey is a barmaid star
Working hard at the Garden Bar,
Attracting punters in from many a mile
Lured there by her "Sirens" style.

Now our Lynsey knows her trade
And never a slip up by her is made,
For she knows all her customers well
So what we all drink, she can tell.
Although this can go to her head
For you maybe given something instead,
I was recently offered "Blonde or Bitter"?
But drink John Smiths, so she missed a sitter.

That though was a one off lapse
As had taken her eye off the ball perhaps.
But as she laughed her "gaff "away
Our Croydon girl was heard to say,
In Anglo Saxon language, very plain
She would never get caught by me again.
But that's not fair, I'm only having a crack
As lovely Lynsey will welcome me back!

Away from the Garden Bar I hear
She makes great cakes, when not pulling beer.
But others must eat her cakes with vigour
As she retains her stunning figure.
With no sign of an eating swell
Although she is a great cook as well.
So she must keep herself in line
When guzzling up her bottles of wine.

Thus I think we're all lucky to see
Her smile, and ready to serve you and me,
So having got this all off my chest
I gladly admit, Lynsey's one of the best!

--ooOoo--

Laurie Wilkinson

To Be or not To Be?

It's so easy to love a beauty
Or a handsome hunk of man,
When their years are still worn well
So you grab them when you can.

The passion levels are high
With erotic mood in the air,
As you move to ravish each other
Without a thought or care.
Maybe this will last a while
Or perhaps stretch to years,
But unless there is commitment
It will all end in tears.

For as time keeps moving on
The years will take their toll,
And looks that were so wholesome
You will find that age has stole.
Possibly also adding illness
With a change of demeanour too,
So the person you are left with
Is not the one you knew.

And after the notorious ten years
When nature mutes her call,
To frolic deep into the night
And now hardly bother at all.
For familiarity breeds contempt
With a boredom at very least,
And whilst a truce is fashioned
Special moments may have ceased.

So you may now have a decision
That you don't really want to make,
Do you cut the ties that bind you
Or carry on for old times sake?

--ooOoo--

Laurie Wilkinson

Gratitude

Thank you mum and dad
For the gifts you bestowed on me,
I'm just sorry it took me so long
The very depth of them to see.

You taught me to count my blessings
Although we were always poor,
But love and happiness prevailed
Of that I was certainly sure.
And though you were not young
At the time that I was born,
You did everything for, and with me
So I could never be forlorn.

I'm told I wasn't always easy
And could play up like a clown,
But you never worried much
Saying that I would soon calm down.

Mum was taken at only seventy three
Though dad had a much longer life,
Which was quite amazing really
After childhood poverty and strife.

But they had a smiling effervescence
Which carried us across life's woe,
Thus again I will thank you for this
As it follows wherever I go.

I wish I could talk to you now
To say thanks again for all your care,
And perhaps reflect you would be proud
Of my achievements I want to share.
Like my degree and career I had
That may have been beyond your view,
And now a three times published poet
That I know is all down to you.

So I say to you many thanks again
For the characteristic traits you gave,
That ensure I will be smiling always
Until I'm put down in my grave.

Laurie Wilkinson

Availing

Smouldering look from the photo
A sort of Mona Lisa smile,
With just a hint of humour
Flitting across the facial style.

So what is behind the mask
And veiled features peeping out?
Like some inverting conjecture
And perhaps self conscious pout,
From this deep inner self
That so very few get behind,
As that is only for the trusted
Sharon will decide are kind.

Therefore you must go gently
Whilst on the fragile outer path,
But looks can be deceptive
And may disguise a wrath
Slow to surface maybe,
Though not to be ignored
By the careless or unwary,
Who need to be insured.

For behind this slender form
Crowned by gorgeous tumbling curls,
I suspect are hidden depths
She for chosen few unfurls.
Thus I have stepped carefully
As it's prudent to hesitate,
To earn respect and friendship
Before let inside her gate!

--ooOoo--

Laurie Wilkinson

Touch

Apparent in a wonderful vision
This sight for sore eyes to see,
A woman with alluring looks
Who seems very attractive to me.

Of course nature plays her tricks
Upon the poor male species of life,
Which causes many an intrigue
And more than a little strife.
For the lovely sirens in our view
Cause bubbling emotions in man,
That instil a profound sense of need
To kiss and cuddle them if he can.

Now with a gentle caress or touch
Emotive sensations come alive,
To those soft pressures and strokes
On which our bodies thrive.
So don't be shy of natures lead
Into temptation with a natural wish.
When signs and permission glow,
Brush her skin with a subtle kiss.

Then if this is received with pleasure
And perhaps an encouraging gasp,
Do not delay or be bashful
Or magic may slip from your grasp.
So continue with sensual movements
With words of complimentary love,
To ensure that you and your lady
Will soar to the heavens above.

--ooOoo--

Hypnotic Dance

Everyone has a love song
Or poem deep in their heart,
Maybe you can never sing it
But knowing it is a start,
To begin to seek your dream
Of a love you never found.
So you slowly start to move
Towards that luring sound.

Hypnotic rhythms stealing thoughts
When drawn forward in a trance,
To the person of your desires
Who is wanting you to dance,
While cuddling up so tight
Before kissing that loving face
You now know waits for you,
At that magic, sensual place.

So with bated breathe and hope
That was never there before,
You prepare to meet your muse
Of which you're really sure.
Because this love song tells you
Something great is coming,
And while you wait and tremble
Loves music is now strumming.

Therefore you sway and wallow
In loves mood that's oh so deep,
Without the slightest movement
To awake you from your sleep!

--ooOoo--

Laurie Wilkinson

Tricky Vicky

Vicky works down my local
Adding bit of glamour to the bar.
But alongside Scott and George
She doesn't need to go too far,
In making an attractive impression
Whenever she's working there,
Though Vicky does this with ease
No matter how she wears her hair.

For sometimes she piles it up
Other times lets it hang down,
Which greatly changes her looks
That causes me to frown,
As I am easily duped by these
Matters of our head hair.
For unlike Vicky's flowing mop
I have nothing up there.

So Vicky cheerfully serves the pub
Giving a smile as well as beer,
Which "insures" like her job
You want to come back in here.
For Vicky seems very at home
Like going back to her roots,
Wandering around the pub
Looking lovely in her boots.

So on request I pen this poem
As our Vicky asked me to,
But as there are other staff in
I could be writing quite a few.

--ooOoo--

Come Our Tomorrow

I will have all of your love tomorrow
And share our kisses so very sweet,
For we will always have it all
Each and every time we meet.

I will feel your touch tomorrow
As your hands explore my frame.
Saying you've had private moments
But without me, it's not the same.

I will bring you to life tomorrow
As I gently stroke and softly caress
Your body, just as you like it,
When your secret parts I address.

I will fuel your desire tomorrow
To make you want all you feel,
For until it's just the two of us
Those desired heights aren't real.

I will hold you close tomorrow
As we melt our bodies into one,
To feel that glorious togetherness
When we are finally all done.

But I'm coming for you now my love
Coming for you fast as I can drive,
For I have set desire all aflame
And tomorrow may not arrive.

--ooOoo--

Laurie Wilkinson

HUMOUR

Who Goes There?

Remembering passwords can be hard
And also a user name too,
Before gaining any access
On technology owned by you.

But you tap in with a confidence
The word needed to log in,
Though sadly it comes up "error"
For this battle you won't win.
So you try again, so sure you're right
By putting in your word name.
This will surely be the one
But the failure's just the same.

"Forgotten your password?" flashes up
And through gritted teeth you hiss,
"No of blooming course not"
I just like playing this
Stupid and annoying game,
Before I can check my screen
And read all my information,
Though it looks like I'm too keen!

Change your password on here then
And all will be right for you,
But you will need to add your
User name, before this you do,
And successfully pass this test,
That's now making you see red.
So you bash your keys in anger
And watch the screen go dead.

Laurie Wilkinson

"Oh most holy gosh and bother"
You mutter under your breath,
Knowing that it's all your fault
That caused the lap top's death.
For it doesn't want to respond
Whatever trick you try to use,
So it seems like poetic justice
If technology you abuse.

A journey to the repairers
Is now a trip you must make,
Confessing or not your guilt
You had more than you could take,
In dealing with requirements
Of all security names and text,
That you thought would be easy
But you forgot what came next.

So if there is an answer to all this
And to not look like a clown,
It's to say bugger their advice
And write your passwords down!

--ooOoo--

No Hiding Place

At our local swimming pool
You can see many a curious sight.
With lots of lovely young girls,
Whilst other scenes are a fright.

Men wearing tight fitting trunks,
"Budgie Smugglers" for the thin.
Though sadly worn by some "largies"
Having more hanging out, than in!
For it seems a life contradiction
That the larger many folk grow,
Instead of tucking it safely away
They must put it all out on show.

Now I'm not against big sizes
I have a growing waist myself,
But I fervently try to hide it
Not put it on the front shelf.

But back to those swimming trunks
Of varying size of modesty cover,
With the battle of those bulges
Where some really need another
Or much larger piece of cloth,
To keep their harvest all intact.
For hiding mountains behind a stamp
Won't work, and that's a fact!

--ooOoo--

Laurie Wilkinson

Spot of Bother

A crispy blouse or clean white shirt
Are almost certain to attract the dirt,
So however hard you try not to be rude
You will still blot your top with food,
That you observe with great dismay
For it will always happen that way.

But some food types that you chose
Are guaranteed to spoil your clothes,
With a spot here, or a splash there
Despite your best attempts at care,
For with some food it's best to be petty
Like that messy, tricky spaghetti.

So when spruced up so smart and clean
You will make mess that's easily seen,
With blobs and slops down your front
The poorest eyesight won't need to hunt.
And the more you rub and wipe the stain
It will look much worse and still remain.

But men have a problem very grave
If hurrying too much when they shave,
And nick themselves, though not too big
It will still bleed like a stuck pig,
So that you wish you'd left off your top
When your bleeding refuses to stop,
And now you're due to go smartly out
So that being on time is a big doubt.
As you must rapidly change your attire
Your readiness now goes down to the wire,
Till at last again all dressed to thrill
But any chance to stay clean is virtually nil.

--ooOoo--

Laurie Wilkinson

Sunrise Strip

The weather is getting better
And sunshine is coming back,
Which surely heralds the return
Of the famous builders crack,
That greets us from their shorts
Failing to gather everything in.
Looking terrible on the large
And not much better on the thin.

Now our rare sunshine is the cue
For awful sights, if I can be blunt,
With bums showing at the back
And bellies hanging out the front.
Though our builder or tradesman does
Go to work with all his might,
But sadly in too small shorts
That allows rock bottom sight.

Another grotesque view we get
Seen in towns of grit and dirt,
Is when the suns rays come out
The blokes must remove their shirt.
And if that's not bad enough
With exposure of their belly flops,
They disgustingly walk round like it
Inside our stores and shops.

So that is some of the problems
When out the sunshine comes,
Though folks enjoying it is good to see
But not a close up of their bums.
Now I'm not a model icon
Sure my body has it its flaws,
But if exhibitionists can't cover up
It's far best they stay indoors!

--ooOoo--

Laurie Wilkinson

Bears Empty Promise

Who's been eating our porridge?
Ted n Beth would like to know,
When they come in for breakfast
After smelling food on the go.

But the porridge has all gone
The saucepan is scraped clean,
For though teddy noses smell it
There is nothing to be seen.
Only an empty dish and spoon
Still placed upon the table,
By another empty cookery jar
With "Porridge" spelt on the label.

This does not please our famous bears
Not one little bit at all,
For they're just beginning to rue
Not getting up on their first call,
When they decided to lay back
And have another little sleep.
With no thought of repercussions
That now makes them weep.

For the breakfast cook has done
And won't be making any more,
Of that delicious porridge
That most teddies will beg for.
And although the penny's dropped
They should have jumped out of bed,
Their dad has scoffed the porridge
So they will go without instead.

But Ted n Beth have both learned
A precious lesson so sublime,
And will make sure they're ready
For their breakfast the next time!

--ooOoo--

Laurie Wilkinson

Double Vision

I went into this village pub
For I was dying for a beer,
But I was very soon to learn
Not to ever come in here.

For I stood at the bar patiently
With a throat dry as a bone,
Despite coughing and shuffling
It seemed I was all alone.

But then a noise behind the bar
Caught both my ear and attention,
And with a very surprised eye
Saw the cause of service retention.
For the Landlady and barman both,
Were doing what comes naturally,
So I realised to my dismay
Neither would be serving me!

Now in a huff I went round the side
And into the other bar,
But saw a barmaid and Landlord
In a clinch that went too far.

So storming out for another pub
That would hopefully quench a thirst,
I tripped over two copulating dogs
And furiously upon them burst,
With barely contained fury now
Complete with an angry frown,
I threw the randy dogs inside
Saying your ruddy sign fell down!

--ooOoo--

Laurie Wilkinson

Black Socks

The guy was all ready for the sun
I mean this man had it all.
A shirt to find your way home with,
With shorts just a bit too small.
A baseball cap perched on his head
While a neck chain said he rocks,
He had a smashing pair of sandals
But Oh, with jet black socks!

These were pulled high up his legs
Right beyond his calf,
So despite all your best efforts
You couldn't help but laugh.
Now I'm not against black socks
Of course they have their place.
In black shoes and dark trousers,
But in sandals they're a disgrace.

So our man swaggered in the sun
Taking off his trendy hat,
Revealing scant hair but a pony tail
Hanging on his shoulder like a rat.
Now I really don't wish to be cruel
But it was this that made me wail,
Though a close call belly laugh
Between black socks and pony tail.

Though we do live in a free country
And can wear what you will or won't,
But with black socks in open sandals
It's far better that you don't !!!

--ooOoo--

Laurie Wilkinson

32

Coffee Capers

The coffee machine lurks ominously
In many a canteen, cafe or bar,
Waiting for use by the unwary
Though they won't get very far.

For these coffee dispensers are computers
Or they may just as well be thus,
As they baffle many a would be user
Who should work them without fuss.
But these things have a devil side,
That reduce many to unhappy fears
Of frustration at their incompetence
To get some coffee without tears.

So go boldly up to them and serve
Yourself coffee as marked by the guide,
To uncertain victims putting cups down
Who watch as the coffee pours outside
Of that awaiting cup of yours
Placed just where told you "oughta".
But when you push the button again
It only fills your cup with water!

But this only happens if you can see
How you think this conundrum works,
For there are many levers and taps
That all have their different quirks.
So you just stand in embarrassment
And shame not knowing what to do,
But fear not for there is consolation
As most are beaten just like you.

--ooOoo--

Laurie Wilkinson

Bears Fan Club

Ted n Beth want a fan club
Saying that they're famous bears,
Having been in a National paper
That only the best poetry airs,
And it featured them travelling
With their passports and a bag,
Across the world and locally too
Very happy to fly the flag.

They also say, pointing out to me
They've been in all my three books,
And that Ted is very brainy
Whilst Beth has dark good looks.
They're in a poem in book one
But in the second, star in three,
But in only two poems in third book
Though they say that's down to me!

Thus they think a fan club is right
For bears of their public standing,
Who at anytime now they believe
Will on top of the charts be standing,
Because of their vast popularity
When folks see them laugh and smile,
In many pictures and photos
Together, or alone for a while.

But Ted n Beth are a double act
Seeing themselves as a team,
And to have a Ted n Beth fan club
Would be like living their dream,
Of sharing all of their adventures
And tricks they play on their dad,
They know is The Psychy Poet really,
But the best author they've ever had!

--ooOoo--

Laurie Wilkinson

Bladdered?

Gosh my bladder is so full
It won't hold another drop,
But I'm driving with my legs crossed
And can't find a place to stop.

My concentration is steadily going
I can barely think straight at all,
And I must answer this urgent message
Or I will soon be sitting in a pool
Of escaping heated liquid,
Crying that it needed release.
So I must relieve myself somewhere
For mind and body are craving peace.

I then turn off into a back street
But no handy trees or fields are here.
Thus I get on my knees behind the door,
So my actions are not clear
To anybody who looks my way,
Who can't see if I'm there or not.
And again I count my blessings
That I have no need to squat!

Laurie Wilkinson

Oh what is it with our bladder?
That it remains calm without a need
To be emptied for many long hours,
But other times requires top speed.
Then it seems you have only just been
To do what your body commands,
And before you can relax carefree
It again makes its demands.

Psychologists think they have the answer
And are certain that they know,
The more you think about your bladder,
It will increase the need to go.
But I'm not convinced that's right,
Though it could just be me,
Who thinks the further from a toilet
Will bring on the need to pee.

So that's the conundrum of the bladder
And complex without a doubt.
But one thing we know for sure is,
That what goes in comes out!

--ooOoo--

Laurie Wilkinson

Anybody There?

Is there anybody out there?
Someone who can hear or see,
All those texts and messages
That were sent to you from me.

Oh, you thought they were statements
So there was no need to reply?
Even though I had asked questions
Like how was that and why?
But nothing came back from you
If that reason is to be believed.
And don't you think it's good manners
To acknowledge they were received?

Yes I know that you are busy
There's not enough hours in the day.
But does it really take so long
To quickly reply back and say
Thanks for my communications
And you will say more later on?
For I am not clairvoyant
So must guess where you have gone.

But just ignore my protestations
For I know I'm not alone,
In making these observations
And I'm really sure you will atone.
Though of course I know for certain
That I will hear you loudly yelp,
And be inundated with your contacts
The moment you need my help!

--ooOoo--

Laurie Wilkinson

Slow Hand George

There's a barman at the Garden bar
And "slow hand George" is his name,
For no matter if you're full or gasping
His manner's just the same.

No special favours or service
As he ponderously runs the bar,
With little acceleration shown
No matter who you are.
So many a dry throat croaks
Whilst waiting in his queue,
And you really fear you'll die here
Before he even gets to you.

But be re assured it's not personal
For every punters thirst will fall,
In the time "ol' slow hand" serves you
That's if you're even seen at all.
So as he shuffles to the end
Where the glass washing's done,
You wait until he comes back
Thinking a marathon he's run!

Though there is always hope here
That he will serve you in a trice,
As he has chatted up security
To run and get his ice.
And of course another trick
To keep slow hand from sin,
Is knowing you will get served
When the barmaid wanders in.

But I mustn't be too scathing
About slow hands lack of go,
For as you hopefully walk in
George will always say hello,
And give a welcome smile
With occasional clever look.
But I must confess I like him,
And he's even bought my book!

Teddy Friends

Our Ted n Beth have many friends
With whom they share their time,
Chatting away, and laughing with some
While with others they sing and rhyme.

Big Ted is a soft cuddly protector
Like a giant minder watching out,
For any dangers or problems seen
That can make him growl and shout.
For although a big fluffy bear
He can talk and knows what's right,
In the world of his teddy friends
That he always keeps in sight.

Now Sleepy Bear just slumbers on
And keeps her teddy eyes shut,
Though on occasions she will peek
And do things sweet as a nut.
But the other bears don't all know
Of Sleepy Bears little game,
Thinking she just dreams forever
And always looks the same.

But I have seen and caught her
Moving and adjusting her bow,
Though she didn't see me looking
So still thinks that I don't know,
Of her little tricks and secrets
Which she keeps from other bears.
Hoping that she fools them
And leaves to their own cares.

Laurie Wilkinson

Ted n Beth aren't caught though
And know exactly what she's at,
But think she's really cute
So agreed to leave it at that.
Brown Bear watches at the window
For he is always on his guard,
To see who is living near us
Or is walking up the yard.
Though he knows friend from foe
And maybe watches for a ghost,
But he mostly recognises callers
Like the man who brings the post.

Thus Ted n Beth are very lucky
To have such lovely friends,
Who care and look out for them
And follow all their trends.
But though Ted n Beth are happy
With how they spend each day,
At the slightest talk of travel
They can't wait to get away!

--ooOoo--

But

Though only a very small word
It can work just like a tut.
When people say one thing
And then change it with a 'but'.
For example you may often hear
"I don't want to pry or be rude"
But then they proceed verbally,
To be offensive and intrude.

"I really didn't want to say anything
But then just felt I had to",
And they continue to comment
On all that you say or do.
Another example is semi praise
That can initially sound nice,
Like "I thought you were very good
But you need to practice once or twice".

So if people are thinking something
And know what they want to say,
Why the need to use the 'but' word
Before saying it anyway?

"Oh and it's really not my business
But thought I should make you aware",
And then go on and advise you
Whilst fixing you with a stare,
Which shows just that they think
The opposite to what they said.
For believing it does concern them,
You should do it their way instead.

So that is my little comment
And the subject I will shut,
For I have nothing more to say
And don't want to upset you, 'but'!

--ooOoo--

Laurie Wilkinson

Escape Hatch

The passenger was extremely large
Nothing else that I could say,
While to my horror and alarm
Seemed to be heading right my way.

I sat there transfixed with terror
At the fate I was about to meet,
When twenty plus stone of flesh
Crashed down in the next seat.
I must have looked quite mortified
As "excuse me" the gargantuan said,
Whilst I could only contemplate
Being squashed until I was dead.

For surely I could never survive
Like this for a nine hour flight,
As increasingly onto my space
Crept his massive spreading might.
And thinking it could not get worse
He had to raise his arms as well,
Releasing to my shocked dismay
A rancid, body odour smell.

So increasingly crushed and gassed
My face surely registering my pain.
But a miracle was about to occur
Right here on this very plane.

For a sweet voiced stewardess
Took pity on my grief and woe,
And completed my narrow escape
Saying to the plane's rear he could go,
Where there were several empty seats
That this fat man could spread over.
Thus rendering me with great relief
At being a lucky wild rover.

--ooOoo--

Laurie Wilkinson

Guest Right

I've been invited back to Radio DGH
To be live on their Christmas show,
So I am honoured, and a little bit thrilled
But don't let that Phil Masters know.

For if he feels I am too eager a guest
And have started to get stars in my eyes,
I fear that repercussions will start
With my having to pay for the mince pies.
Not to mention a charge for having a seat
As I struggle to reach the mikes,
With a threat to cut me off mid flow
For in his studio Phil does as he likes!

I have also been reliably warned
That the studio reflects seasonal cheer,
So this made me even more concerned
About who will be buying the beer.

Tinsel and bells adorn the inner sanctum
That is "hospital radio's" little home,
And so I worry about the festive mood
Even if I read from my latest tome.
Though this I am more than happy to do
For I like my weekly poetry call,
Also reading them out live today
With a Merry Christmas wish to you all!

--ooOoo--

Fly Past

Flying creatures can be aggravating
And get you extremely mad,
Buzzing around and landing on food
Like an airborne "Jack the Lad".

Some can give you a sting as well
Filling many folks with dread,
That they will get a nasty prick
As they zoom around their head.
But flapping your arms all about
Won't work and can make you grieve,
For you will get stung for sure
If you trap one up your sleeve!

But what is it about those little flies
That makes us lose our wit?
Perhaps it's because they like poo
With a passion to roll in it,
And then eat some for a meal
For that's exactly what they do,
Ensuring that when they land on us
It can make us want to spew.

Though one special annoying thing
Is that persistent little fly,
Who however many times you swat
Just determines not to die.
So you flail your hands manically
Trying to give it a fatal crack,
But when you think you've got him
The blighter comes flying back.

So the war on this tiny air force
Can go to extreme lengths,
Although it's a very unequal fight
With very different strengths.
For you do your level best to kill
Your miniature battling foe,
Who when you think that you've won
Will do a fly past, and then go!

Laurie Wilkinson

44

Philippa

Philippa shares a proud surname
Of a famous sailor named Drake,
Though I don't think she has sailed much
So no further comparison can make.

But Philippa has her own ways
With brown eyes and compelling stare,
That will fix you to the spot
As her enthusiasms she'll share.
For she loves writing her poems
Some very deep and others drear,
Though you can never doubt at all
That these ideas are quite sincere.

Delivered in a broad, heavy accent
That from Glasgow she did bring,
Her poems are sometimes complex
So you must listen to everything.

Although sometimes that's hard,
As Philippa will whisper low
On occasions as she reads them,
But in the end you will know
The crux of the very dark lines
She mostly likes to write,
That takes you off with demons
And often to a ghastly sight.

Though lately all that has changed
With perhaps a new attitude,
For many of her new poems
Are quite near the mark and rude.
But not in the way of outrage
For after all is said and done,
It is another way she writes now
And is just her sense of fun!

--ooOoo--

Laurie Wilkinson

Three Limericks

1

There was a woman from Barrow
Whose eyes were extremely narrow,
But they would shoot open wide
If receiving inside,
Anything the size of a marrow!

2

A lady was filled with dread
About being tricked into bed,
So to keep safe from that
She would never lie flat,
And now walks about on her head.

3

There was a man from Woking
Who spent all his life joking,
But he had failed to see
The folly of picking on me,
So now the bugger is choking!

--ooOoo--

Late

The clock is ticking past the time
That you had agreed to meet,
And nobody has called round yet
So you begin to fidget in your seat.

You start to think and ponder
If the right time is in your head,
But you can only convince yourself
Of the time that you both said.
So if believing that you are right
Perhaps they must have got it wrong,
Though one thing now is certain
Is that you can't wait too long.

For today with all our technology
Any communication is very easy.
With a phone call, text or message,
But getting nothing makes you queasy.
So you start marching all around
Making little circles on the floor.
Whilst getting more worried and anxious
As still nobody is at the door.

Again you ring their numbers
But no answering voice replied,
It just seems you're getting snookered
With everything done or tried.

The agreed time is now well past
And arrangements are up the wall.
Until double checking your diary
And start to feel an utter fool.
For there should be no one coming
Though the agreed time is as you state,
But the answer to your frustrations
Is that you have the wrong date.

--ooOoo--

Laurie Wilkinson

Scott or Not

Down my local is "Scott or not"
As I name his lack of recall,
For if someone's bin in asking
For you, he won't know at all.
So learning who the person was
Or what they had to say,
Will never be known by you
After an hour, let alone a day.

For Scott who forgets has issues
As he puffs upon his pipe,
As he politely tells you now
That he is not a memory type.
So of course I must now wonder
When he cycles off to roam,
And rides his bike for miles
How the hell does he get home?

For a homing pigeon he is not
With an elephants memory,
So please don't leave a message,
If you want to contact me.
Though an idea would be a note
With my contacts on a chit,
But as sure as eggs are eggs
"Scott or not" will then lose it!

But be assured he can always
Pull a pint without delay,
And despite his dodgy recall
He won't forget you have to pay.
Though I'll say Scott has helped me
And in a big way as it goes,
Promoting me, and buying books
Which supports Help for Heroes!

--ooOoo--

Laurie Wilkinson

Tripe and Onions

Tripe and onions, bangers and mash
Even spaghetti bog as well,
These are meals we love to have
But why do we have a need to tell
About everything we eat and drink
On news and social media's view?
For if that is not all enough
We have to see photos of it too!

Here is our lovely meal just served
Doesn't it all look rather grand,
With a photo of smiling faces
Just for fun you understand?
So now a full view of ordered meal
To be scoffed by the wild rovers,
And yes that we can just about take
But not the photos of your left overs!

With shots of half eaten bits of food
Or perhaps a plate that's almost clean.
As it was the best food ever you said,
As if we had all never been
Out for a meal or even a banquet
As that's how your description seems,
To us spectators on media logged
And seeing everybody's dreams.

Though I must admit to my cynicism
Like Mister Shakespeare's touch.
For if everything is so wonderful
Why do you have to say so much?
About the very best of food
That only you seem to have had.
So come on you can't really believe,
We don't all think you a little sad?

--ooOoo--

Laurie Wilkinson

REFLECTION

Moment in Time

The world spins on its axis
Night darkens the light of day,
Summer follows winter and spring
Our times were made that way.

Yet we go on in our existence
Even if we want to or not,
For however much we fight it
We mostly have the life we've got.
For as we continue on our road,
Days will come that bring our turn.
To have some suffering to bear,
From which we need to learn.

For as our loved ones die on us
Others will come as we see them go.
Replaced by babes newly born,
In natures continuous flow.
So enjoy what you have now
For as long as you possibly can,
Because there is no certainty
Of the time scale given to man.

Waiting for exactly the right time
To do all that you want to do,
May catch you out very badly
And be totally denied to you.
Thus best appreciate it all now
Even if the truth hurts and numbs,
For however hard to accept it
Sometimes tomorrow never comes.

--ooOoo--

Laurie Wilkinson

Cradle to the Grave

A lilting voice from the past
That will affect you like no other.
Bringing love and goose bumps too,
For it can only be your mother.

The one who always from your birth
Stood by you with no quaking,
Though inside she cried bitter tears
If bad decisions you were making,
Or was given cause to be upset
At your failure to return the love,
Which will always be too late
After she is taken to live above.

For a mother always looks with pride
At your first shaky steps to walk,
Across your rocky paths in life
Since she first helped you to talk.
Thus had also been there for you
From that cradle to the grave,
Watching out for all those dangers
As your soul she tried to save.

So when others reject and doubt you
Your doting mother will be there,
To ensure she can protect you
With unconditional loving care,
That first began when as a child
You needed succour and a kiss,
Given with uncomplaining lips
You will always sorely miss.

A lilting voice from the past
You will remember all your years,
Though may not always appreciate
Until her passing brings your tears.
So while you have her, be ever nice
To your solid embracing fir,
Who whatever heartbreak you cause
Will still put you first, before her.

Laurie Wilkinson

Poets and Scrollers

The news comes flooding into our lives
From places nationally or world wide.
Amusing, frightening or tragically sad,
Yet from it all, it's hard to hide.

Graphic images often feature large
As the world comes to our door.
Exposing to us the very worst of man,
As the news channels try to explore
All aspects of life to fully scrutinise
Under a glaringly microscope.
Making you angry, laugh or cry
Or possibly give up all hope.

So how do we deal with a bombardment
Reeking havoc on mind and senses?
Confronting us with with manic thoughts
That causes mass upset and offences.
Some will merely just look away
Denying they have seen, or know it,
But others take it all to heart
And most likely they're a poet.

For poets tend to write on things
With strong thoughts and burning phrases,
That encapsulates and rams it home
To the indifferent who it amazes.

So having seen it put into words
These ostriches or rock and rollers,
Still prefer to avoid any sympathy
By being just news reel scrollers.
Who turn a blind eye to sad events
Until something happens to them too.
When a poet will then come forward
To comfort their tragic view.

--ooOoo--

Laurie Wilkinson

Heartfelt

A positive mind yields a happy heart
For troubles come, and some go slow.
But if you are steadfast in your way,
You can help any heartaches go.

For all of us will have challenges,
We must do our very best to meet
With strongest resolve we can find,
Or get knocked right off our feet,
By seismic shocks that shake you
And possibly cause you many tears.
Though if you tackle these heroically
You may have better future years.

For a positive mind yields a happy heart
And helps make troubles seem smaller,
Thus meet them in a courageous way
And you certainly will walk taller.

For I feel I'm living proof of this
Being a very optimistic man.
Though I have had many trouble too
But met them the best way I can,
For even if I lost sometimes
I always stood back up again,
Which certainly was best for me
Although of course I felt the pain.

So onwards in life and upwards
We must make our merry way,
Because even if sad times prevail
We can still fight another day.

--ooOoo--

Living Well

If you're thirsty you may go to the well
To quench your thirst with a drink.
And you may do it automatically
Without ever stopping to think,
About how the water got there
Or the need to put something back,
Because the water may soon run dry
If the well is allowed to crack.

For in our world little comes for free
Although plenty will live for this,
By taking out everything they can
And giving help requests a miss.
For they are too busy taking all
It's possible to get lazy hands upon,
Ensuring when it's pay back time
They'll be well and truly gone.

So for us in a concerned majority
Is the need take care of our well
And other gifts passed on to us,
As they are not ours to waste or sell.
When the sacrifice of many others
Gave them up without a cost,
Only a big responsibility of trust
To see they are never lost.

Thus this commitment is now ours
To appreciate and protect this wealth,
Of the things we may take for granted
All the time they're in good health.
But just a little thought and effort
Will see our gifts all safely supplied,
And to know our drinking well is flowing
Will meet our wish after we've died.

--ooOoo--

Laurie Wilkinson

The Spider and the World

The spider lurks in the shadows
And then its web will spin,
Waiting for the world to arrive
Before naively going in.

The world too will spin around
As we mere mortals live our days,
Trying to understand everything
In so many different ways.
With some things we succeed
But others will prove too much,
For that's the way of a complex world
And what we never get to touch.

Meanwhile the hermit like spider
Sits patiently in its thread,
Awaiting for the blind unwary
Who very soon will be dead.
Stuck and trapped quite helpless
Condemned to a gruesome fate,
In the cruel fangs of that spider
Or maybe killed by its mate.

So perhaps there is a comparison
Between the spiders web and man,
Who in their very different ways
Just get by the best they can.

With one sitting in a subtle trap
As for victims it quietly waits.
While we in our world twirl in frenzy
And dread to hear what fates
Or misfortune will befall us,
With nerve ends all stretched taut,
Before blundering through our lives
And in webs of deceit get caught.

--ooOoo--

Laurie Wilkinson

Ghost

I have my own personal ghost,
You can't see him but he's there.
When I'm alone I talk to him
And so my existence I will share.

We discuss things when life's difficult
And I don't know what to do.
I am not too sure if he does talk back
But It's like another persons view,
On what to do, or what to say,
Or maybe how best to proceed.
So I get an inner confidence
And my echoes advice I heed.

This ghost of mine is real to me
And he even has a name,
Though it's probably no great surprise
That his and mine are the same,
For when talking I will use it
As I would address a human friend,
Knowing my ghost will be around
Until my days come to an end.

So I guess now that I am aware
That It's my conscience not a ghost,
But to me it doesn't matter
If having integrity I can boast!

--ooOoo--

Only You

Most of the successful people you meet
Won't have let grass grow beneath their feet.
But it's not all about making money,
More of creating your world that's sunny
And makes you smile across your ways,
And grin back at whatever days
Don't sit well or rest with others,
For the fact is we're not all brothers.

So get up and get your ideas on
For tomorrow they could all be gone,
And disappeared down the slippery slope
Leaving you frustrated without hope
That you can ever move yourself,
To gain prosperity and wealth.
But do not worry too much on this
For money is not the only bliss.

Now cast around this world of ours
Where a negative thought always devours,
But if you have your health and brain
There is little that can restrain
You from doing what you will,
Ensuring happiness soon must fulfil
Your heart and all you do,
For there's no point in being blue.

So to just finish and be very exact
It all comes down to a simple fact.
And in this there's no need for debate
That you can a success create.

--ooOoo--

Profit and Loss

It's said that cheats don't prosper
But I'm not so sure that's true,
For some nasty people seem to win
Whatever evil that they do.

So unperturbed they continue
To sneak a bit here and there,
And sometimes more than a little
Not that they seem to care.

Mind, some profiteering is legal
As with "Bankers" and their perks.
Risking our money for their gains
Within strange law that lurks
Beneath the light of decency,
As becomes the common man,
Who prefers to do a good job
For fair pay if he can.

But more insidious are the people
Who know just what they do,
Cheating and lying without remorse
That always baffles me and you.
So as we watch these villains
Rarely work but take hand outs.
And seem to have no conscience,
Any qualms, or uneasy doubts.

Though I, amongst many others
Watch with frustration at the trend.
To cheat whenever possible, though,
We hope evil loses in the end!

--ooOoo--

Laurie Wilkinson

Railways of Life

If the "good time" train calls at your station
Make sure that you get on board,
For you may never get another chance
After "please mind the doors" is called.

Enjoy this journey and give thanks
For your blessings and good days,
Remembering it could be quite different
And you may travel less happy ways.

For railways of life can be fickle
Also known not to run on time,
And many have mechanical breakdowns
Leaving heartbreaking hills to climb.
So be aware of the many junctions
That any railway tracks may take,
And that you may well be stranded
If flawed travel plans you make.

So "bad time" trains may convey you
To destinations you don't want to see,
With uncomfortable times prior to arrival
From which you cannot break free.

Thus it's always best to map your trip
With all the plans you want to make,
For if your life journey all goes wrong
It could be more than you can take.

--ooOoo--

Birds of Prey

The circling birds were looking
For those weaknesses in you,
Any anxieties or a depression
That they can lead you to.
For these birds are more like spectres
Flying around to seek you out,
To try and make you panic
Or cause worries and self doubt.

So best run and look for cover
If you feel not at your best.
As these circling birds will swoop
And transport you to their nest,
That's a nasty world of darkness
With crushing mental pain.
For if you succumb to your demons
You may never recover again.

How are spectre birds successful
In seeking the vulnerable out?
Maybe they have some inkling
Of any self confidence drought,
That may resonate off your bearing
Possibly seen by a nervous stance,
So beware these spirits will get you
If they suspect the slightest chance.

Thus be armoured in your standing
And don't let these vultures win,
Because any weakness you exhibit
Will likely emanate from within.
So seek a solace and comfort
For any fears or doubt you feel,
As this will gird and protect you
When those flying spectres wheel.

--ooOoo--

Laurie Wilkinson

A Leader and the Pack

Many people have to bunch up
To follow the crowd like sheep.
But for others this is folly
And so to themselves they keep,
Being both confident and able
In their abilities and ways,
And while herds gets bogged down
They will look for better days.

It's said who goes fastest, goes alone
And I guess that may be true.
But the strong leader type
Will always look for pastures new,
Where they seek out opportunity
They mould to satisfaction,
Whilst meanwhile the herd complains
Of their lack of life or action.

Though there's safety in the pack
Jostling along with all the crowd,
Never having to worry much
As lateral thought is not allowed.
So with their minds stagnating
The herd moves slowly on,
But may later rue missed chances
After the prizes have all gone.

So why do people want to lead
With all that added strain?
Though I think many would do so
If they had the choice again.
For while there's company in packs
With not very much to fear,
In that boring cheerless herd
Life is dark and very drear.

Thus the leader makes his way
Continuing to take his chance,
And while he may go wrong at times
His whole life he will enhance!

Laurie Wilkinson

Memories

Oh how well we can remember
The recognition of a mothers love,
Given so free and unconditional
As if sent down from high above.

Oh how well we can remember
The comfort of a big hug,
Like warming before a big fire
Sitting on a thick pile rug.

Oh how well we can remember
The magic of our first kiss.
As we puckered up together
With a handsome hunk or pretty miss.

Oh how well we can remember ,
When we first had too much to drink,
Vowing never to do that again
As alcohol is stronger than you think

Oh how well we can remember
The wonder of when we first made love,
Feeling the intimacy and warmth
As we soared to skies above.

And it's well that we remember
These precious moments of life's thread,
To enjoy them and the memory
Before the time you wake up dead!

--ooOoo--

Laurie Wilkinson

Envy ?

Some people come, whilst others go
A few for reasons I don't know,
Guess it was something I did or said,
That didn't settle well in their head.
But meanwhile I will trek my road
So all are welcome with my load,
While I continue with my life
Mostly wondrous, with little strife.
Thus I will offer a smile or joke,
Though on this some seem to choke.
For I am not always like a saint,
And a colourful life I love and paint.
But do not worry if you fail to see,
That I'm always, and forever me!

--ooOoo--

Days

We count our time and mark it
By the number of our days,
Although this can be deceiving
For they're spent in different ways.
With some people doing nothing
Content to watch the world go by,
But others work or fill their hours
So for them their days will fly.

Though time will always beat us
As like the tide it never waits,
So before we're mindful of it
We are at those proverbial gates!

So looking back at times past
Allows our yesterdays to arrange
Thoughts some will say are foolish
For those days we cannot change.
But perhaps looking back is prudent
With its memories and teaching,
To review and maybe smile
At our actions so far reaching.

Laurie Wilkinson

Thus if those past times are sad
It is best not to mope or dwell,
As we can take lessons forward
So may prevent another hell,
Which perhaps befell our lot
Whether ours or others fault,
But if the learning has gone in
We should not again get caught.

Another concern for some folks
Is having ambitious dreams,
That can change days into nights
And a life not what it seems.
But enjoy and embrace such thoughts
Even if your body they do tire,
For it's a very strong belief
That we need dreams to aspire.

So there is the quandary of life
No matter what you think or say,
For we live in the here and now
And must fulfil the present day.

--ooOoo--

Thought Process

You can dress it up in fancy titles
As "life coaching" or "positive thought",
But if you really make the effort
From your own brain can be wrought,
The motivation and the pathway
To achieve just what you will.
In your own chosen manner
With the necessary skill.

You can get bogged down of course
And not know what way to turn,
But by setting out your plan
It's amazing what you can learn.
Though any wasting of your time
Seems to be a particular trap,
So awareness of any priorities
Will prevent a needless a flap.

But one thing I will acknowledge
As a tremendous help and view,
Discussing all with another
Is the best strategy for you.
Thus how to resolve problems
And to get your process done,
Will be helped in the resolving
For two heads must beat one!

--ooOoo--

Laurie Wilkinson

Dumb Army

Education is a wonderful thing
But on some people clearly wasted,
For many give up the ghost
Before having barely tasted
The wonders and treats in store,
Which will catapult your brain
To contemplate sights and sounds
Like some heaven sent refrain.

But opting out and to decline
Education and gifts of learning,
Appeals to some as much easier
Like the simple life they're yearning.
Though of course this has risks
That are as obvious as a brick.
So although their ignorance is bliss
They will spend life being thick.

Of course being stupid is not illegal
And you can't get jailed for being daft,
But you have to wonder sometimes
How some make it such a craft.
For most of life floats by them
Like water off a ducks back,
And only when it suits them
Will it be noticed what they lack.

Fortunately as we're a free country
You can do mostly as you choose,
So the dumb army will only need
To know the price of booze.

--ooOoo--

Laurie Wilkinson

Just Scene

Life can be a goldfish bowl
Whether looking out or in,
But mostly when stared at
It shows up your every sin.
Or perhaps unguarded moment
When you carelessly let go,
And took a chance for freedom
Not expecting it to show.

Now stripped of all your armour
Where you had safely hid inside,
You must now face the audience
Who your verdict will decide.
So gird up your loins strongly
And stand proudly at the bar,
To show the world your failings
But also how good you are.

For everyone has their secrets
And some little hidden shame,
But those who deny loudest
Will recognise their blame.

Thus be not afraid of the brash
Who so harshly you will try,
As it's their guilt they're washing
So stare them squarely in the eye.
Because soon their gaze will lower
As inside they know it must,
For after all is said and done
We've all given in to lust!

--ooOoo--

Laurie Wilkinson

Sunny Side of the Street

The sun will often shine down
Causing shadows where it meets,
Sides of the way or roadside
But can be sunny on the streets.

So some folk will always strive for
The best place to put their feet,
For they will just seek to be
On the sunny side of the street.
No rain of life must touch them
Or you will loudly hear them bleat,
The injustice of their fortune
If not on the sunny side of the street.

Many trials of life will test us
As to who can bear stress and heat,
Though lots will give up trying
To rest on the sunny side of the street.

But you can find many decent people
That you are overjoyed to meet,
Who don't spend their life seeking
That sunny side of the street.
And maybe you will find some love
With someone oh so sweet,
But this can lead to heartbreak
If they want sunny sides of the street.

So this dismal story covers most
Who just want to run and retreat,
And be self centred and non triers
On the sunny side of the street.

Though life will have more for you
If appreciation of it you show,
Treating the world and people kindly
You'll have sunshine wherever you go.

--ooOoo--

Laurie Wilkinson

One Light Wonders

Accidents are so often caused
By going too fast, or blunders,
But now we have another worry
In the form of "one light wonders,"
Who apart from their bad driving,
Are a big danger in the night.
For with their lights not working
They can play havoc with your sight.

With only one headlight shining
And if the side light's out too,
You can be mistaken into thinking
That a motorbike's in your view.
But of course the blacked out side
Still takes up the same room,
Though of course you can't see that
Storming towards you in the gloom.

And often if bulbs aren't all working
The lights wont be shining right,
So the one main beam that is on
Is far too dazzling and bright.
Thus just to compound the dangers
Of how "one light wonder" drives,
So often too fast and reckless
Until his undertaker arrives!

--ooOoo--

Mister Know it All

It was such a privilege to meet him
For in this world of large and small,
You can meet many different people
But I've just met Mister know it all.

A self confessed man of forty seven
Already portly and with bifocals too,
He looked more my advancing years
But a better man than me or you.

For everything that had been achieved
He'd been there and done it better.
Boasting of his brilliance whilst,
Thinking you believed him to the letter.

Though he did seek confirmation
From his fawning mate called Shaun.
Who nodded puppet like but shyly,
And at most times, quite forlorn.
As I'm sure he was embarrassed
The more elaborate stories became,
Like never losing when gambling
And winning on each and every game.

I must have looked back quite cynically
For have heard fairy tales before,
As he then appeared very anxious
When I edged towards the door.

As when learning I retired very early
Said he could stop work at anytime.
So after I asked him why he didn't
His reply was laughably sublime.
For he had three special life insurances
That would never ever recede,
At which I seemed too disbelieving
On his policies no failing breed.

For this was all news to me
As most stocks and shares move,
Up and down at various times
That many bankruptcies will prove.
But by now I was realising
It was pointless debating with might,
For Mister know it all was certain
That everything he said was right!

So now I was making my excuses
Being desperate to take my leave,
And escape this bragging moron
That no one will ever believe.

--ooOoo--

Laurie Wilkinson

TRAGEDY

Downcast

I see you struggle under the load
The world has decreed you must,
Carry and forever be burdened with
Until your flesh and bones are dust.

The withered look upon your face
Shows up the pain racked mask,
As you blunder on the road of life
Cowered by the impossible task
Of coming to terms with your woe,
Along with shame and deepest sorrow
That you and I know for sure
Will be just the same tomorrow!

What you may ask has fashioned this
To bring a strong person down?
Saddling him with crushing weight
And the wearing of a losers crown.

Well the answer to this is simple
And beware not to watch and judge,
The unfortunate stood before you
Whose guilt and ire wont budge.
For he suffers mental illness
Though his earlier times were kind.
But dark satanic thoughts and shapes
Now play havoc with his mind!

So he must project a physical norm
When clothed by harvests of depression.
That despite all his efforts and aims,
It only compounds regression.

--ooOoo--

Laurie Wilkinson

End of the Line

Deepest, darkest thoughts now
Are descending on your mind,
As you look back on the years
You see that life's not kind.

Your aching, limping body tries
To keep up with commands,
Put on it by necessity now
That keeping alive demands.
So within your failing shell
With senses closing down,
You creep about a little world
Wearing a pain filled frown.

Is this what it has all come to?
After a life of battling hard,
To keep wolves from the door
And trying to not be scarred
By asking too much of others
Who require a lot from you.
But that is all forgotten now
Despite the good you do!

Oh how the early times passed
Without care or downcast thought,
Of what was in future's store
However hard you fought.

For everyone takes for granted
That life will be good to them.
And suffering that others feel,
Will never crush and condemn
Their own puny, precious world,
That ageing and depression fills,
Before the final curtain falls
And the precious life blood spills!

--ooOoo--

Lambs and Guns

I am naked except for my clothes
No match for knives, bombs and gun.
You can kill me anytime you want
For my only defence is to run.

You are fully armed to your teeth
A veritable arsenal moving on legs,
So you can slaughter and maim at will
No matter how much your victim begs,
As they relax, carefree on a beach,
At a cafe, or maybe a music hall.
Thus your foul war on the unarmed
Ensures that only the innocents fall!

Creeping, slithering, making your plans
Hiding in shadows behind a locked door.
Disgusting cowards, strapping on bombs
For your sick, ambushing war.

Thus you avoid, and wont bring to combat
Any trained and well armed man.
So you stick to putrid sewers,
And attack like only scum can.

For I am naked except for my clothes
No match against knife, bombs and gun.
You can try to kill me anytime you want,
But it's not my only defence, to run.

So stalk our free world, trying to see
Easy targets like lambs, unaware at play,
Your brainwashed mind and smoking gun
Will never earn a winners sway.

--ooOoo--

Laurie Wilkinson

One in Three

Love and laughter may sprinkle around
With no real problems for you and me,
But we must always be aware of the fate
That will befall every one in three.

For our lives can change in a trice
When the world sends us a test,
To deal with tragedy, failure or loss
When we are forced to do our best,
To keep our chins up and smile
And face the world with fragile pride,
That may fool many, and maybe you
Until you realise you're dying inside.

As a blackness so dark falls all over you
With no pinprick of light in your pit,
So you blunder about and don't even try
Whilst every sinew begs you to quit,
And perhaps shuffle off this mortal coil
That right now seems most appealing,
For even if you do try to fight back
You're overwhelmed by a darkest feeling.

Where has all this come from you ask?
But in truth you may never know,
How you are reduced to anxiety tears
And constant feelings of death and woe,
That will affect many now in their lives
As if have swallowed a depressive pill,
For you have become one in the three
Who learn the trauma to be mentally ill.

--ooOoo--

A Coward and the Innocents

The coward crossed the playground to the school
His twisted mind determined to break every rule
Of decency, love and peace in Dunblane,
This cursed, pathetic man; Hamilton by name.

In a place for primary age children there
He sprayed random shots without a care,
Of the sick, sad outcome of his goals
To slaughter and maim those sweet young souls,
Who had full lives in front of them to live
And whole generations of love to give.
Now stolen by this inadequate man's worst
Act, that ensures he is forever cursed!

Prevented from his vile intent on young child's
His perverted mind was now lost in wilds
Of deserts, swamps and putrid sewers,
His sick revenge as parents hearts he skewers.
For destruction of the innocents he seeks
So in a school gym, cowardly havoc he wreaks,
With four loaded pistols he guns down all
That have the tragic misfortune of his gall.

Thus because of him many children now lay
Bloodied and dead on that foulest day,
For the innocent lives of seventeen were taken
By this twisted madman now always forsaken.
On that unlucky thirteenth March in 96
When for his contemptible end he picks
Out sixteen babes and a brave adult,
Removed from life by his bullets bolt.

So now twenty years past we look back in pain
With no sure rhyme or reason for his gain,
Of an accursed name reviled forever
Whilst his blessed victims lie in love together.

--ooOoo--

79

Laurie Wilkinson

Across the Way

We nearly all have a cross to bear,
They can be big, or sometimes small.
Some will have lots, others not many
Though the lucky have none at all.
Thus we stagger along our roads
With these burdens on our back,
Of varying degrees, each one of us
Trying to keep to the beaten track.

Some people's crosses you never see,
For they wear pain behind a mask
Of a ready smile or flippant joke,
Inside though, crushed by their task.

But others will keep telling you
How hard their life with no reward,
Despite every help they won't pass on
So will never earn happy accord.
How then I wonder is this all agreed
With life's loads unfairly shared?
And unkind people let off scot free
When for others they never cared.

But those diamond folks of our world
Who care for everyone else first,
Will carry such a big and heavy cross
You think their heart must burst,
Though somehow they stagger on
Managing to help many foe or friend.
So you come to realise their worth
Knowing they'll win out in the end.

--ooOoo--

Playtime Sorrows

There is a pained look on your face
And consternation in your heart,
For you have so many regrets now
You don't know where to start,
At looking back across your years
That you always said were fine.
For it was easy to placate then
Only now those times won't shine.

Your decisions concerning children
Or not to travel about the world,
Are now starting to nag at you
As your true feelings are unfurled.

But of course you can't go back
And anyway you made your choice,
So it's very hard that it upsets you
With that anguished inner voice,
That laughs loudly at your grief
Giving you a depressive stance.
Not there when you mocked others
Without once taking any chance.

So yes it may have been different
If more risks you chose to make,
But sitting safely on your fence
Any excitement you did forsake.
Thus now you are all alone
With no past wonders to review,
Or a family to spend time with
For it was only ever about you.

--ooOoo--

Laurie Wilkinson

Questions of Innocence

Why did you have to kill me
At my young and tender years?
Maiming and killing others too
Replacing laughter with their tears.

Why did you have to kill me?
You didn't even know my name,
And why murder all the others
Whose religion is just the same
As what you now claim yours is,
Or is it really more a love of war?
That spreads blood and slaughter
But only makes you scream for more.

So religions now all stand together
Different creeds you want to separate,
Some with backgrounds just like yours
United now with the ones you hate,
Brought together in huge revulsion
At your sick, barbaric act,
That will only work against you
With more unity, that's a fact.

But why did you have to kill me
And not give me any chance?
As you blew yourself up beside me
Without the slightest second glance.
Do you think that you'll find peace
In any life after your bomb burst?
Because wherever you do land
Your soul is forever cursed.

--ooOoo--

Alone in the Mirror

I am alone in the mirror
This face I've come to know,
That's been staring back at me
From so many years ago.
But that face has changed now
Though the expression is the same,
For it has seen much of life
And situations you can't tame.

This face has looked on loss
So tragic it creased with pain,
While trying hard to smile out
As inside the heart was slain.
Inner traumas rocked the soul
Which nearly split the seam.
Causing untold agony but,
Outside the face would beam.

So laughter which we cherish
Has cracked the outer look,
Though these smile fed lines
Will belie the times it shook,
With mirth, and sometimes grief
As it was worn across the years,
That eroded pristine youth
With many of life's fears.

So that cruel mirror on my wall
Reflects the good and bad,
Showing with lines and wrinkles
All the years of life I've had.
But I'm not ashamed of this
Please don't be taken in.
For though sometimes I force it,
Years drop off when I grin.

--ooOoo--

Laurie Wilkinson

Full Circle

Some things in life are pre ordained
As we're put on earth without a vote,
And only accident of birth
Will decree the make up of your coat.
The fine fabric of affluent families
Or threadbare rags of the poor.
Whatever manner we are born to,
We will all die, that's for sure.

So then it comes to the middle bit
Between our birth and death.
Our screaming arrival in the world,
And then our last rasping breath.
How then will we make out
And deal with life's many tests?
Working as hard as we can,
But in between having rests.

For all work is not a good thing
Neither is it to be totally lax,
So we must have moderation
Before our credibility cracks.

Enjoy each moment of this time
For to waste it is a crime,
So no moaning or cursing luck
As very quick we can come unstuck,
Regretting the things we didn't do
In courageous moments, so very few.
Then all too soon you're at that gate,
Where all hopes may evaporate.

--ooOoo--

Spirit Level

We strive for a balance in our life
But it is very hard to keep
Across the stresses of each day,
With times to laugh and some to weep.

But copious tears are dangerous
If you continually have to cry,
For one day you will be tearful
And find your tears have all run dry.
The same goes for a heart that grieves
When troubles against it clutch,
So beware even the stoutest heart
Will die if it bleeds too much.

Over the years we lose our strength
As age and troubles prolong.
Thus all our worries accumulate
Whilst we are not so strong
To resist the raging currents
That our weary bodies batter.
For the passing years bring woes
That in youth just didn't matter.

So yes, we can be all cried out,
Our milk of human kindness gone,
But somehow we must find the nerve
To get up and carry on,
When every nerve and sinew screams
At you in an anguished cry,
To give up, although you can't,
Let go until you die!

--ooOoo--

Laurie Wilkinson

Two Way Mirror

It's often easy to see the problems
Those things that aren't quite right,
And do not seem to be working,
Seen with the gift of second sight.
So judge away and cast the stone
For the target is an easy one for you,
Not having to rectify what's wrong
And much easier to say than do.

For creeping mists of darkness come
When tears of inner pain fall,
So you may just see the anguish
But can't ever know it all,
And how the battering of turmoil
Erodes away to expose the nerves,
Left raw by the nagging vibes
Of the doubt that worry serves.

Look in and make your observations
On what you think is seen,
But how can you make judgements
On where you have never been?
Or to understand the pressures
And the frustrations of a change,
To something you knew completely
But now it just seems strange.

For the world will bring in heartaches
And condemnations with the years.
That can distort life grotesquely,
So we are left with bitter tears.

--ooOoo--

A Rock and a Hard Place

Like two barricades standing firm
Or obstacles you can't move aside.
However much effort you put in,
I know this, because I've tried.

On one side you have a history
Going back with more than time,
And although you wish to be free
It's too steep for you to climb,
Mocking your best endeavours
To reach the freedom at the peak.
Reducing you to mediocrity
Against which you cannot speak.

So the other side looks easier
And you give it your best shot,
For the rewards look massive
But easy to move it's not.
Though still pushing against it
Believing you can succeed,
For you have a renewed vigour
But it just makes you bleed.

So condemned to stay trapped
Between this rock and hard place.
You finally combust and blow
It all away without a trace.

Thus in the ensuing carnage
The very worst that you might do.
You hear an anguished crying
That could only come from you.

--ooOoo--

Laurie Wilkinson

Help Harvey

Harvey is a lovely Spaniel dog
And only five years old,
So we hope you will help him
When his story I have told.

For at only a young nine weeks
His femur he did break,
Which has now led to arthritis
So the pain he struggles to take.

With all insurance money spent
He must have a new hip now.
Though this will be very costly
And so he hopes you will endow
His fundraising and collection pot,
On his "gofundme" donation scheme
Organised by his human mum
And a large caring team.

Now Harvey is a loving family pet
And dealing with his pain is plucky,
Also only having sight in one eye
No way is he called Lucky.
For his boisterous friend Jager
Caused the accident to his eye,
And now he also needs another hip
But you can help him if you try.

With a target of five thousand pounds
To get Harvey free from pain,
Any donation for his new hip you make
His eternal love you'll gain.

--ooOoo--

Shock

Gasping, choking, struggling to breathe,
Head spinning fast, brain trying to believe
And take in the message you hardly heard,
With eyes full of tears, your vision blurred.

Inside you there's dust, instead of your heart
And searing agony, as your soul's ripped apart,
Still trying to comprehend the painful shock
From the words your ears tried hard to block,
Whilst knowing you'll walk in the desert of dread
Now you've been told, your love affair's dead!

--ooOoo--

Easy for Steve

I see behind your nervous smile
And hear the words I can't believe,
As you try to hug and placate me,
But please don't call me Steve.

I see the different way you look at me
And your covert actions can't deceive,
For although you put a good act on
You still went and called me Steve.
So best you make your decision
Although this we cannot retrieve,
In fact you can do what you like
But just don't call me Steve.

For I have observed your jumping
Each time you catch your sleeve,
As you dress yourself in haste
Because I'm not a bloke called Steve.
But that shouldn't worry you much
Or give you any cause to grieve,
Now that your treachery is exposed
With that low life you call Steve.

Thus turn those shifty eyes aside
For my sight is not so naïve,
And get yourself well away from here
With the man whose name is Steve.
But I will issue you a warning
So strong that you must perceive,
Having betrayed once, you will again.
And my name's not bloody Steve!

--ooOoo--

Standing on the Corner

I have to say I quite like a beer
Served in any shape or measure,
But drinking on some windswept road
Will not give me any pleasure.

Yet a regular sight on our streets
Is a little huddle of forlorn folks,
Desperately flapping about for warmth
And puffing away at smokes.

Now I must confess to have never
Got caught up in this trend,
Making you cough while clogging lungs
As you now stand frozen on a bend.
Why does it make you so desire it
And leave friends inside all warm?
As you head towards the smoking patch
To be all alone or in a swarm.

Though it wasn't always like this
People could just puff away at will,
And while smokers were very happy
So many others just felt ill.
Having been in the midst of nasty
Mini mushroom clouds from those,
Who blew smoke about with impunity
That left us ashtray smelling clothes.

Thus now the tide has turned a bit
Making smokers have to stand outside,
For even if they lurk under cover
The smoke detector makes them hide.
But I am no great misery now
Out to end what folks call fun.
So go and stand out on the corner
For smoking over us, isn't done.

--ooOoo--

Laurie Wilkinson

Sticks and Frames

However sturdy was your prime
In old age you're not the same,
For many a fit and healthy man
Now has to use a stick or frame.

Even worse if you let things go
In matters of your future health,
Smoking and gross indulgence
Will certainly help age's stealth,
As it creeps up steadily in time
Quicker the less exercise you do.
For often when it comes to life
Most decisions are down to you.

Pretending you're too tired or ill
For any activity or a game,
Will surely accelerate the need
To use a walking stick or frame.

Sitting for hours inert in a chair
When you can move about much more,
Allows our bodies to slow down
Though of that you won't be sure.
So makes excuses as you will
That you're unlucky and not to blame,
If misfortune should condemn you
To have a stick or walking frame.

But whether any of this is true
And should you hide from any shame,
Maybe it would have taken longer
To require your stick or walking frame.

--ooOoo--

Laurie Wilkinson

Broad and Narrow

Narrow escapes or a very close call,
In our life we will see them all.
A second thought on a hubby or wife,
That may save you a lot of strife.

For once they have you in the bag
They may never cease to nag,
Despite all the good things they say
And may even tell you that they are gay.
So always best to try the wares
Removing chances of shocks downstairs,
Or any other places in the house
Where you must play cat and mouse,
Before you can safely shut the door
On more surprises still in store.

Some narrow escapes we won't know
For if they don't happen, or even show,
When we're about, and are around to see
What could have affected you and me.

So best count the blessings in our luck
When fortune seems to pass the buck.
And to us, we a nasty experience miss,
Thus we continue in ignorant bliss.
For there are many who get their share
And others too, that they have to bear.

But some exceptions to that rule,
Are those coming from a nasty school
Of life, who really do not give
A hoot for others who caring live.
So accept narrow escapes in your day
Whilst praying that they'll always stay.

--ooOoo--

Laurie Wilkinson

Autumn of Love

The autumn of our love is descending
No more to feel our heartbeats blending,
It's fading fast, the end it is near
Our love shares the fate of nature each year.

I never now see that spark in your eye
That was always there, however shy.
So I can tell that we're going wrong
Soon to be singing that saddest song.
That haunts all loves that have lost,
Leaving us to count all the cost
Of wasted time, and wasted dreams
Replaced by our souls agony screams.

The autumn of our love is descending
No more to feel our heartbeats blending.
That loving magic is there no more
Laying instead nearly dead on the floor.

It never seemed to us we'd fail
To live forever in loves glow,
But people and times will always change
And turn into strangers you don't know.
So best to stand up, tall and square
With your freshly painted smile,
That you know will see a lonely road
Hurting and aching, mile after mile.

Thus many a face will turn away
At your look of contagious gloom,
Whilst rushing back to lover or spouse
In a frantic bid to save their doom!

--ooOoo--

Laurie Wilkinson

Swan Song

The swan glides serenely across water
But paddles furiously away below,
Although it isn't really obvious
So you might not even know.

Unlike some manically busy people
Who always seem out of breath,
Dashing and charging about
Almost keen to meet their death.
So they could learn from the swans
And their balance of activity spent,
Who with their graceful exercise
Reach all destinations of intent.

Now back to our frenzied man
Or woman, as some are the same,
Racing about the world in fear
With worries they cannot tame.
Thus wearing out weary limbs
And putting pressure on the heart,
Which struggles with their panic
That seems so quick so start.

For our bodies are well designed
To resist and cope with strain.
But will obviously be pressurised
If overworked time and again,
With very little peace or rest
From this continued stress,
Of which very few manic people
Have the courage to confess.

So take your lesson and learn
The swans relaxed life song,
For surely the people who can't
Won't be around for very long!

--ooOoo--

Laurie Wilkinson

Appendix

Feedback on my poetry recounts that many people like to work out the meanings of my poems for themselves, and even attach their own personal experiences and thoughts. I think that is wonderful, but for other folks who like to seek my reasons and explanations for them, please review my comments below.

As I tend to write spontaneously and often on subjects that have really emoted me, I will mostly "nail my thoughts in", so most of the themes are self – explanatory. The poems listed in this appendix are the less obvious topics and thoughts, but please feel totally free to add any personalisation or meaning that they have for you individually.

Jigsaw : When love comes together

Kiss : A magic we all seek and enjoy

Return Flight : A love from the past you always remember

Lost for Words : Frustration of a language barrier

To Be or not To Be : A dilemma of love

Gratitude : A tribute to my fantastic parents and all they did for me

Who Goes There? : My frustration with technology and trying to "log in"

Black Socks : One of my pet hates and amusements

Coffee Capers : The trauma and trials using coffee machines

Anybody there? : My annoyance of people who don't reply to messages

But : People who will use the word after stating they won't say anything

Tripe and Onions : A friend asked me to write this on our shared bemusement of people who must post photos of their food leftovers!

Moment in Time : On the circle of our lives

Cradle to the Grave : On a mothers unconditional love

Poets and Scrollers : That some people care about the world, others don't

Heartfelt : Positivity in your life works best

Living Well : Count your blessings and appreciate what you have

The Spider and the World : That our own little world can be very different to other peoples

Birds of Prey : Try to be as strong as you can

Days : Maximise your life

Thought Process : On people who "life coach" others but maybe not themselves?

Just Scene : People who always judge you and others but not themselves

One Light Wonders : On the increasingly dangerous number of vehicles with light faults

Mister Know it All : A man who "descended" upon me in a bar, and "big" in every way

Downcast : The crushing effect of mental illness

End of the Line : On growing older

Lambs and Guns : My response to terrorist atrocities in 2015, culminating with the Friday 13th November bombing and shootings in Paris

One in Three : That we may all fall prey to mental illness

The Coward and the Innocents : Dunblane killings, twenty years on

Across the Way : That life isn't always fair but must be lived whatever

Playtime Sorrows : Avoid regrets in later life

Questions of Innocence : My disgust at 2016 Brussels suicide bombers

Alone in the Mirror : Recognition of getting older as life goes on

Full Circle : A balance in life we should all try to find

Spirit Level : The need for resilience in older life

Two Way Mirror : That we don't always see what people are dealing with

A Rock and a Hard Place : Sometimes in life you can't win

Easy for Steve : About peoples betrayals that we might see at times

Standing on the Corner : A lament and message for smokers

Sticks and Frames : Look after your own health as much as you can

Swan Song : Manically charging about isn't always best

Requested and welcomed by an increasingly appreciative audience, Laurie Wilkinson aka The Psychy Poet, produces his fourth and larger book in only 3 years, again proudly offered by My Voice Publishing.

Continuing the successful format of his previous books, Laurie scans the world with a curious eye for his observations. He watches happy and tragic events, making poetic recordings of life and behaviours of people in everyday settings and stages of life.

Again embracing expansive subjects that brought glowing accolades for previous books, Laurie tackles romance, with an increasing erotic verve, frustrations of life, grief, terrorism, mental illness and of course features those roguish bears, Ted & Beth.

Laurie's new poems here will again entertain and amuse, whilst a resonant effect will induce mixed emotions about our lives and experiences as he describes them in powerful and down to earth manner.

The author is again confident this book has something for everybody and that the reader will enjoy as his journey continues.

Life Scenes

Life's scenes are acted out
Right before my eyes,
So I can't help but notice
The careless and the wise.

Thus will have my feelings
About all that I have seen,
And will put them into words
So others know what I mean.

For poets have passionate thoughts
Put into burning words and verse,
As I observe the world's scenes
That are better or much worse.

Lightning Source UK Ltd.
Milton Keynes UK
UKOW03f1522150517
301152UK00001B/21/P